## Animals in My Backyard
# EARTHWORMS

Aaron Carr

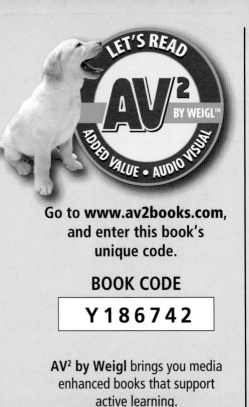

LET'S READ

**AV²**
BY WEIGL™

ADDED VALUE · AUDIO VISUAL

Go to **www.av2books.com**, and enter this book's unique code.

**BOOK CODE**

Y 1 8 6 7 4 2

**AV² by Weigl** brings you media enhanced books that support active learning.

AV² provides enriched content that supplements and complements this book. Weigl's AV² books strive to create inspired learning and engage young minds in a total learning experience.

# Your AV² Media Enhanced books come alive with...

**Audio**
Listen to sections of the book read aloud.

**Video**
Watch informative video clips.

**Embedded Weblinks**
Gain additional information for research.

**Try This!**
Complete activities and hands-on experiments.

**Key Words**
Study vocabulary, and complete a matching word activity.

**Quizzes**
Test your knowledge.

**Slide Show**
View images and captions, and prepare a presentation.

# ... and much, much more!

Published by AV² by Weigl.
350 5th Avenue, 59th Floor  New York, NY  10118
Website: www.av2books.com  www.weigl.com

Library of Congress Cataloguing in Publication data available upon request.
Fax 1-866-449-3445 for the attention of the Publishing Records department.

ISBN 978-1-62127-211-3 (hardcover)
ISBN 978-1-62127-215-1 (softcover)

Printed in the United States of America in North Mankato, Minnesota
1 2 3 4 5 6 7 8 9 0  16 15 14 13 12

122012
WEP301112

Senior Editor: Aaron Carr    Art Director: Terry Paulhus

Weigl acknowledges Getty Images as the primary image supplier for this title.

# Animals in My Backyard
# EARTHWORMS

## CONTENTS

Meet the earthworm.

It is long and round with a soft body.

Its body is made up of many rings.

With many rings, its body can stretch out long or squeeze in tight.

7

Each ring of its body
is covered with many tiny hairs.

Its many tiny hairs
help it crawl through the ground.

It digs tunnels in the ground.

The tunnels in the ground help plants grow.

It comes out of the ground when it rains.

When it rains, its tunnels
in the ground fill with water.

It eats dirt as it digs through the ground.

As it digs through the ground, it finds all the food it needs.

It has no eyes or ears.

With no eyes or ears,
it has to use its other senses.

It can often heal itself
when it is hurt.

When it is hurt, it may grow new body parts.

If you meet the earthworm, do not touch it. They are very important for plants and other animals.

If you meet the earthworm, stay away.

21

# EARTHWORM FACTS

These pages provide more detail about the interesting facts found in the book. They are intended to be used by adults as a learning support to help young readers round out their knowledge of each animal featured in the *Animals in My Backyard* series.

**Pages 4–5**

**Earthworms are long, round animals.** Earthworms are a type of small, soft-bodied animal that lives in soil. They are invertebrate, which means they do not have a skeleton. There are more than 1,800 species of earthworm. They originally came from Europe, but can now be found in North America and western Asia.

**Pages 6–7**

**The earthworm's body is made up of rings.** Earthworms are a type of *annelid*, or segmented worm. These worms have bodies made up of many ringed segments called *annuli*. The largest earthworms can have up to 150 segments. Earthworms are usually about 3 inches (8 centimeters) long, though some Australian earthworms can grow more than 11 feet (3 meters) in length.

**Pages 8–9**

**Tiny hairs help earthworms move.** Each of an earthworm's segments contains tiny hairs, called *setae*. The earthworm uses these tiny hairs to move and burrow underground. First, the earthworm stretches its body forward. Then, it uses the setae to grip the ground. This allows the earthworm to pull itself forward.

**Pages 10–11**

**Earthworms dig tunnels in the ground.** During the day, earthworms burrow underground, digging tunnels through the soil. Earthworms usually stay close to the surface, but they can dig as deep as 6.5 feet (2 m). They play an important role in the ecosystem. Their tunnels allow air and water to pass through the ground where they feed plants and help the soil sustain life.

**Pages 12–13**

**Earthworms come out of the ground at night.** For this reason, they are sometimes called night crawlers. While above ground, earthworms search for food to eat. They also leave their underground burrows at times of heavy rain. The rain causes their tunnels to flood, forcing them above ground. One type of earthworm found in Asia is known to climb trees to escape rain.

**Pages 14–15**

**Earthworms eat decaying plant matter found in soil.** As earthworms dig through the ground, they ingest soil. The soil then passes through the length of the body while it is digested. Waste is released from the opposite end of the body, allowing the earthworm to continue burrowing. Scientists think earthworms may ingest their own weight in dirt and food every day.

**Pages 16–17**

**Earthworms do not have eyes or ears.** They rely on other senses to move around and find food. Instead of eyes, earthworms have light-sensitive spots on different parts of their bodies. To help make up for a lack of sight and hearing, earthworms have a highly developed sense of touch. They also rely on smell and taste.

**Pages 18–19**

**Earthworms can often heal their injuries.** Unlike most animals, the earthworm can regenerate, or regrow, parts of its body. Depending on the species, earthworms can regenerate lost body segments. Most species can regrow lost segments in the tail end of the body. However, the belief that cutting an earthworm in half will result in two earthworms is false.

**Pages 20–21**

**You might find earthworms in your backyard.** Earthworms can be found in almost any kind of soil that contains enough organic material to support their diet. This means they can often be found in backyards, schoolyards, and other public places.

# KEY WORDS

Research has shown that as much as 65 percent of all written material published in English is made up of 300 words. These 300 words cannot be taught using pictures or learned by sounding them out. They must be recognized by sight. This book contains 51 common sight words to help young readers improve their reading fluency and comprehension. This book also teaches young readers several important content words. These words are paired with pictures to aid in learning and improve understanding.

| Page | Sight Words First Appearance |
|---|---|
| 4 | the |
| 5 | a, and, is, it, long, with |
| 6 | can, in, its, made, many, of, or, out, up |
| 8 | each |
| 9 | help, through |
| 11 | grow, plants |
| 12 | comes, when |
| 13 | water |
| 14 | as, eats |
| 15 | all, finds, food, needs |
| 16 | eyes, has, no, other, to, use |
| 18 | often |
| 19 | may, new, parts |
| 20 | animals, are, away, do, for, if, important, not, they, very, you |

| Page | Content Words First Appearance |
|---|---|
| 4 | earthworm |
| 5 | body |
| 6 | rings |
| 8 | hairs |
| 9 | ground |
| 10 | tunnels |
| 14 | dirt |
| 16 | ears, senses |